I AM

Written By: Wilhelmine "Willow" Bellevue

Illustrated By: Book art

I AM

ISBN: 978-0-9975589-3-7
Library of Congress Control Number: 2023907259

INTRODUCTION

Dear Readers,

Grab your parent, guardian, or loved one with you as you read this devotional book! Together, you can talk about daily devotions and their definitions. Read the definitions first to know what the words mean when you come across them. Reading along with a loved one by your side will make this devotional even more special!

I wrote this book so that you know that you can speak to God and hear from God daily. One is never too young to seek, hear, pray, or experience God. Jeremiah was called by God when he was a young boy. Jeremiah also thought he was too young to experience God and to be His prophet. God told Jeremiah; I know what you can do because I created you. You can do this! I will tell you what to say, and you will say it.

Jeremiah 1:5 (The Voice) says,
"Before I shaped you in the womb, I knew all about you Before you saw the light of day, I had holy plans for you."

God understands our emotions and what makes us sad, mad, and happy. He also knows our strengths and weaknesses. If God knows all of this about us, we should trust Him. My first experience with God was when I was a young child. At ten years old, I was scared of the dark and too embarrassed to share this with anyone. I used to hate going to the laundry room because it meant I had to walk down into a dark basement.

One day, as I stood on top of the stairs, I heard an inner voice speak to me and say, "Say, nothing shall harm me in the name of Jesus Christ, Amen."

I did not know where this voice came from, but I felt better after hearing it. I listened to the inner voice, stepped down the stairs, and said, "Nothing shall harm me in the name of Jesus Christ, Amen." With each step I took, I became confident that God was watching over me. I went into the laundry room, threw my clothes in the hamper, and then ran up the stairs saying, "Nothing shall harm me in the Name of Jesus Christ, Amen!"

After that day, I realized God was close to me. I saw God as a Father who would coach me and be ready to give me a much-needed hug. I felt safe knowing God even cared about the things I had hidden away from everyone else. From that day on, I saw God as Abba, a super-loving daddy. When I call Father God Abba, I picture Him carrying me in His arms with a big smile. I do not have to act tough when I call on Him; I can be me. Saying Abba to Father God is also a way of me saying to Him, "I need you by my side, I love you, and I trust you." Abba means Daddy in Aramaic and is another term for Papa, and Pa. Abba's voice can come to us like an inner voice. As a child of Abba, you will know His voice when you hear it. My relationship with Abba became stronger after hearing and listening to Him.

After reading each devotion with your parent, guardian, or loved one, take a few minutes to pray and tell Abba what that devotion meant to you. Take a minute or two to journal how you apply that day's devotion to your life. I pray this book will help to draw closer to Abba. I also pray you will be more confident with what you see, hear, or know in your spirit.

Willow

DEFINITIONS

Abba- Abba is an Aramaic word that means "God the Father." It also means Papa and Pa.

Sources:
Biblehub.com: *https://biblehub.com/greek/5.htm*
Blueletterbible.org: *https://www.blueletterbible.org/search/Dictionary/viewTopic.cfm?topic=*
ET0000008,HT0000006,IT0000016,KT0000003,NT0000006,VT0000002,BT0000013

Scriptures: Romans 8:14-16, The Voice, "If the Spirit of God is leading you, then take comfort in knowing you are His children. You have not received a spirit that returns you to slavery, so you have nothing to fear. The Spirit you have received adopts you and welcomes you into God's family. That**'s** why we call out to Him, "Abba! Father!" as we would address a loving daddy. Through that prayer, God's Spirit confirms in our spirits that we are His children."

Conscience: A God-given ability to know right from wrong.

Source:
Biblehub.com: *https://biblehub.com/greek/932.htm*

He/His/Him- When referring to God, we always capitalize the H in He, His, and Him. In Exodus 20: 1-21, God shared with the Israelites 10 commandments (rules) He wanted them to live by daily. In the third commandment, Exodus 20:7, God told the Israelites to honor His name. He did not want them to use His name lightly, jokingly, or badly. God still demands this respect from us. Out of respect for God, we capitalize the H in His. The same rule applies when we write He and Him about God.

Scripture: Exodus 20:7, Message Bible: "No using the name of GOD, your God, in curses or silly banter; GOD won't put up with the irreverent use of His name."

Holy Spirit- The Holy Spirit has many characteristics. He is the third person in the Trinity (Father, Son, and Holy Spirit). The Holy Spirit is also a teacher and reminds us of the scriptures. He is a comforter who is there for us when we feel alone, sad, or mad. He is an Advocate; He stands up for us. Sometimes The Holy Spirit looks like fire, and other times, a dove. The Holy Spirit may sound like wind. The Holy Spirit gives us the power to accomplish things and to pray.

Scripture: Luke 3:22, The Message Bible: "The Holy Spirit, like a dove, descending."

Scripture: John 14:26, God's Word Translation: "The Comforter, The Holy Spirit, whom the Father will send in My Name, He will teach you all things, and remind you of all things that I said to you."

Scripture: John 14:16, God's Word Translation: "I will ask the Father, and He will give you another Helper who will be with you forever. That Helper is The Spirit of Truth. The world cannot accept Him because it doesn't see or know Him. You know Him because He lives with you and will be in you."

Scriptures: Acts 2:2-3, The Message Bible: "Like a strong wind, gale force—no one could tell where it came from. It filled the whole building. Then, like a wildfire, The Holy Spirit spread through."

Scripture: Acts 1:8, The Amplified Bible: "You will receive power *and* ability when The Holy Spirit comes upon you."

Jesus Christ- Jesus Christ is the Son of God. Jesus is the second person in The Holy Trinity. Jesus died for our sins so that we may have a close relationship with God and not be separated from Him (God) forever because of our sins.

Scripture: John 3:16, New International Version, "For God so loved the world that He gave His one and only Son, that whoever believes in Him shall not perish but have eternal life."

Jesus calls Himself **The Sent One**. Jesus was sent to heal us from our sicknesses. He was sent to free us from things that weigh us down, like sadness, anger, bad habits, and other things we can't get rid of on our own. Jesus came for those who were rejected. Jesus also came for those who have suffered a loss or experienced hard times, abuse, heartbreak, loneliness, and more. Jesus came so that we could live in freedom, peace, and joy.

Scripture, Luke 4:18-19, The Amplified Bible, "The Spirit of The Lord is upon me (Jesus Christ, The Messiah) because He has anointed [set apart] Me to preach the good news to the poor. He has sent Me [Jesus Christ]) to announce the release (pardon, forgiveness) to the captives, and recovery of sight to the blind, to set free those who are oppressed (downtrodden, bruised, crushed by tragedy) to proclaim the favorable year of the Lord [favorable meaning special blessings, special gifts, special grace or chances]."

Jesus calls Himself the I AM. Jesus has always existed. He was with God from the beginning of time. Jesus is all-knowing; He knows everything. He is Almighty and Omnipotent, which means Jesus can do anything. Nothing and no one is stronger than Jesus, not even death. Jesus is Omnipresent. Omnipresent means He is everywhere at the same time.

Scripture, Revelation 1:18, The Amplified Bible, "I am the Alpha and the Omega [the Beginning and the End]," says the Lord God, "Who is [existing forever] and Who was [continually existing in the past] and Who is to come, the Almighty [the Omnipotent, the Ruler of all]."

Kingdom of God- The rules of Heaven. We are called to have a heavenly mindset, which means to live in peace, love, and obedience to God's word.

Sources:
Biblehub.com: https://biblehub.com/greek/932.htm
Britannica.com: https://www.britannica.com/topic/Kingdom-of-God

Scripture: Romans 14: 17, **WeyMouth New Testament**: "For the Kingdom of God does not consist of eating and drinking, but of right conduct, peace, and joy, through The Holy Spirit."

Visions- Visions are like dreams; they feel very real. In a vision, you can see things others cannot see; this may happen while you are awake or when your eyes are closed. God speaks through dreams and visions.

Scripture: Joel 2:28, International Standard Version: "Then it will come about at a later time that I will pour out my Spirit on every person. Your sons and your daughters will prophesy. Your elderly people will dream dreams, and your young people will see visions."

TABLE OF CONTENTS

DAY ONE:
I AM COURAGEOUS!

Think about a time when you were too scared to do something or go somewhere; this can be anything. Were you ever fearful of sharing your thoughts with your classmates, meeting a new group of people, or even trying out for a team? What made you feel scared? Take time to write your thoughts down.

As human beings, it is normal to feel scared, nervous, or fearful. As children of Abba, we are called to push past our fears because Abba is by our side. When God called Joshua to be a leader He first told Joshua to be strong and courageous.

Focus Scripture: Joshua 1:7, The Message Bible
"Haven't I commanded you? Strength! Courage! Don't be timid; don't get discouraged. GOD, your God, is with you every step you take."

We get courage by speaking Abba's word and believing it. Joshua was told not to be scared because Abba was by his side. Joshua probably said something like this to himself as he went to battle, "I will not be scared. I am strong and courageous. I got this! God is with me! He said I can do it!"

Make it personal and say to yourself: I am strong and courageous. I will be courageous with school, schoolwork, sports, friends, going to new places, meeting new people, speaking up, going to doctor and dentist visits, or anything that may make me feel uncomfortable. Abba is with me in every step I take. I am a mighty warrior.

You may or may not feel strong and courageous right away, but the point of saying this is to build your faith. Even if you don't feel it does not mean you are not strong and courageous. You are strong. You are courageous. The more you say it, the more you will believe it! The more you believe it, the more you eventually feel it.

Fill in the Scripture:

Joshua 1:7, The Message Bible

DAY TWO:
I AM ACCEPTED!

Have you ever had someone, not like you? Have you ever just not fit in with a group of people? Have you ever wished you were accepted or liked? Take a few minutes to write your thoughts.

It hurts when people push us away. The feeling of hurt that we feel when this happens is called rejection. It is important for us to pray to Abba when we feel this and to focus on His thoughts about us. Throughout David's lifetime, he always had someone who did not like him, fought him, told lies about him, or just wanted him gone. David also experienced rejection from his family. Read the scriptures below about David and his conversation with his brother:

1 Samuel 17: 28-29, New Living Translation says,

"But when David's oldest brother, Eliab, heard David talking to the men, he was angry. "What are you doing around here anyway?" he demanded. "What about those few sheep you're supposed to be taking care of? I know about your pride and deceit. You just want to see the battle! "What have I done now?" David replied. "I was only asking a question!"

David was shocked and annoyed about his brother's attitude towards him. David may have even felt rejected, but he did not let that stop him from fighting the Philistine Giant, Goliath. David won his battle against Goliath because he self-cheered and reminded himself of Abba's love. David continued to cheer himself up and remind himself of Abba's love throughout the rest of his life.

Focus Scripture: Psalm 139:17-18, New Living Translation
"How precious are your thoughts about me, O God! They cannot be numbered! I can't even count them; they outnumber the grains of sand! And when I wake up, you are still with me!"

Make it personal and say to yourself: I am accepted! Abba loves me and has many good thoughts about me. Abba likes me and knows who I am. Abba will always be my friend and always accept me; He will never leave me. I will not focus on those who reject me. I will not change for others to accept me. I will continue to be the best me Abba has called me to be. I will focus on those who love me. I will focus on the special gifts Abba placed inside of me. I will focus on the great things I can do! I am enough. I am loved.

Fill in the Scripture:

Psalm 139:17-18, New Living Translation

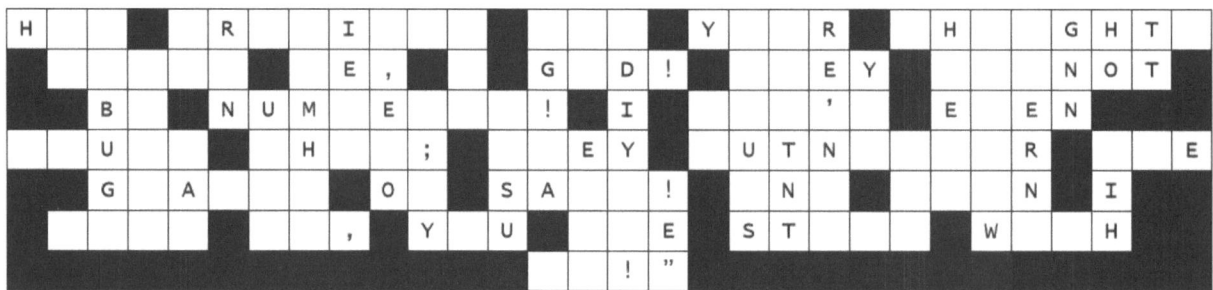

DAY THREE:
I AM MOVING FORWARD!

Think about a time when you did something or said something you were not supposed to do or say. How did you feel afterward? It is a good thing when we feel bad after doing something wrong because that means we are listening to our conscience.

God knows we will fall short or fail at some point, but it is important to move forward. Moving forward means first asking Abba for forgiveness. Admit to Abba what you did wrong and ask Him to show you how you can do better next time. Other times, moving forward means forgiving ourselves. It is possible to be upset with oneself for making a mistake or causing a mess. Forgiving oneself means saying, "I forgive me. I know better for next time, and I will take this as a learning lesson." Forgiveness means letting go of shame, sadness, and disappointment. Even if others may not forgive us, we must know that as soon as we ask for forgiveness, Abba forgives us.

Before becoming a Christian, Paul used to punish Christians in horrible ways. After becoming a Christian, Paul did not allow his past to make him feel small, sad, shameful, or unimportant. Paul served Abba confidently and started each day fresh, knowing he was not perfect. Take a few minutes to forgive yourself and others. For example, write down, "I forgive _____ for _____. I will not hold a grudge against them. I choose to let it go."

Focus Scripture: Philippians 3:13, The Amplified Bible
"I do not consider that I have made it my own yet, but one thing I do: forgetting what lies behind and reaching forward to what lies ahead."

Make it personal and say to yourself: I am forgiven! Abba forgives my sins. I will take responsibility for my actions. I will learn from my mistakes. I will not blame others, even if they are wrong. I will not talk badly about myself. I choose to forgive myself, and I choose to forgive others. Abba has given me the victory over bad behavior, being mean to others, not forgiving others, lying, not listening to adults or my parents, and anything I know is wrong. Abba has given me the power to act, speak, and listen better. Abba has given me the power to move forward in victory.

Fill in the Scripture:

Philippians 3:13, The Amplified Bible

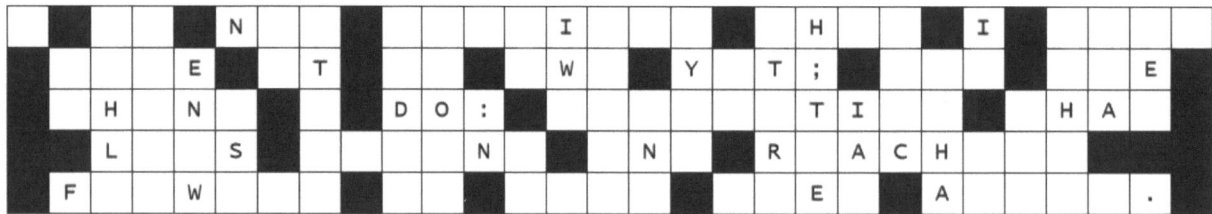

DAY FOUR:
I AM SMART!

What does the word smart mean to you? If you describe someone you think is smart, whom would you describe? How do you feel about your level of smartness? What we think about ourselves does matter. Psalm 23:7(The Amplified Bible) says, For as he thinks in his heart, so is he [in behavior]". This verse says people will act out what they are thinking. So, if someone is always thinking angry thoughts, the person will act angry, like being mean to people. If people think sad thoughts, they will act sad, like crying or walking with their heads down. If someone thinks," I am not smart," guess what will happen? You guessed it! The person will not make smart decisions. Being smart means learning, thinking, planning, and making good decisions. Smart is about more than just studying and getting good grades. What if you studied and did not achieve the grade you wanted? Does that mean that you are not smart? No! It just means you have to try a different way of studying or learning the material.

Corinthians 2:16, The Amplified Bible, says,

"We have the mind of Jesus Christ, Abba's Son, "But we have the mind of Christ [to be guided by His thoughts and purposes]."

We can make good decisions, create strategies, and have The Holy Spirit to help us. We are smart because we have Abba, we have the mind of Christ, and the power of The Holy Spirit. We can ask Abba for His power and the mind of Christ for studying for a test, drawing a masterpiece, reading a book, writing an essay or a book, taking a test, planning an event, performing well at a play, playing an instrument, playing well at a game, dancing, or singing well in front of a crowd. Take a few moments to write down the areas where you are smart and want to be even smarter. For example, write down, "I am smart in _____. Abba, give me the wisdom to be smarter with _____."

Focus Scripture: 2 Corinthians 2:16, The Amplified Bible

"We have the mind of Christ [to be guided by His thoughts and purposes]."

Make it personal and say to yourself: I am Smart! I have the mind of Christ Jesus. I am strategic; I think ahead. I am a good decision-maker. I create formulas and solutions. I am a problem solver. I have a great memory. I excel in all my studies; The impossible is possible for me. Abba gives me His strength and confidence. I am a faithful learner. I have the confidence to learn and understand challenging information. I can study, learn, read, sing, dance, play, write, draw, and (add anything you need help with here). I can do all things with Abba's power and with the mind of Christ.

Fill in the Scripture:

Corinthians 2:16, The Amplified Bible

DAY FIVE:
I AM AT PEACE!

When you think of the word peace, what comes to mind? What does peace look like, sound like or feel like? When you are at peace, you know you are okay. Peace feels like protection, like being under nice warm blankets. Peace can smell like something sweet or calming. Take time to write down a time you felt at peace. For example, "I felt at peace when_____."

Abba gives us peace when things are going right and when things are challenging. We will need Abba's supernatural (Abba's special peace) when we have a sick loved one, a hard time with our families, fear of the unknown, or more. It can be hard to hold on to Abba's peace during difficult times because it is easy to focus on what we see rather than on Abba's peace. Abba knows how hard life can be at any age. Abba sent His Son, Jesus Christ, so that we can have peace through the hard times.

In John 16:33, The Amplified Bible, Jesus told His followers,

"I have told you these things, so that in Me you may have [perfect] peace. In the world, you will have many troubles, but be courageous [be confident, unmoved, be filled with joy]; I have overcome the world." [My conquest is accomplished, My victory abiding.]"

Abba is so good that He does not want us to wait for everything to be perfect before experiencing His peace. Abba wants us to have His peace and joy now! We also have to know Abba works everything out for our good. Sometimes, we may not like how Abba does things, but Abba knows the future. We should be at peace knowing; He makes decisions based on how it will work for our good. We can always ask Abba for peace, and He will give it to us. We can keep His peace by focusing on how He loves us, is with us and will never leave us, and has good plans and thoughts for us.

Focus Scripture: John 14:27, The Amplified Bible

"Peace I leave with you; My [perfect] peace I give to you; not as the world gives do I give to you. Do not let your heart be troubled, nor let it be afraid. [Let My perfect peace calm you in every circumstance and give you courage and strength for every challenge.]"

Make it personal and say to yourself: I am at peace! Abba has given me perfect peace for my heart, thoughts, and body. I will not allow this (say what it is that is troubling you) to take away my peace. Nothing surprises Abba. Abba is working everything out for my good. I am at peace knowing Abba hears my cries. Abba hears my prayers. I am at peace with how Abba answers my prayers, even if not how or when I would like Him to answer them. I am at peace knowing Abba will not leave me; He is with me. I am at peace knowing Abba has given me the power, strength, and joy to get through this difficult time. I am at peace because I have the victory. I am at peace because Abba loves me.

Fill in the Scripture:

John 14:27, The Amplified Bible

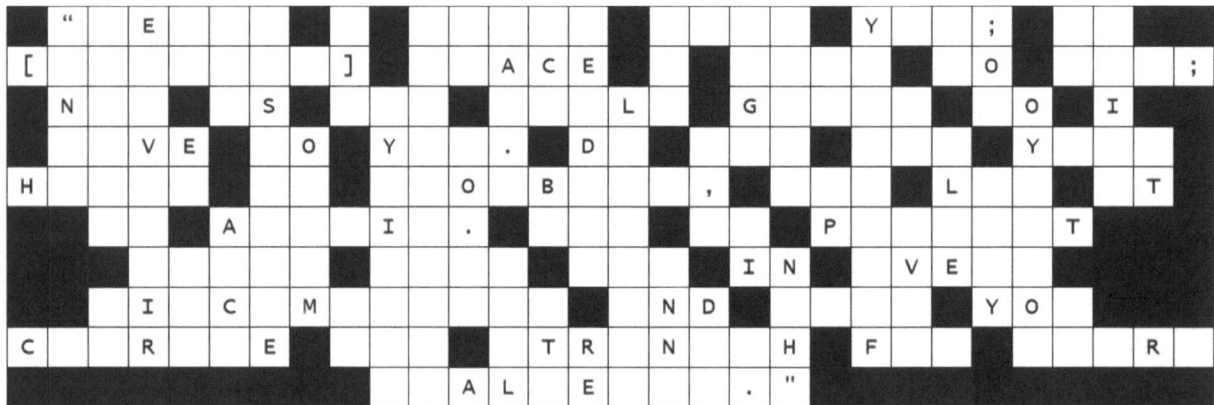

DAY SIX:
I AM HEALED!

Feeling sick is not fun. Sometimes, when people are sick, they lose their appetite, they may want to sleep more often, and other times, they can 't sleep. When people are sick, doing what they usually enjoy is hard because of pain or weakness. Other times, people can feel sick when sad, hurt, or angry for long periods. Abba wants us to be healed from all our sicknesses; this includes cuts, bruises, headaches, broken or sore bones, stomach aches, colds, dry skin, asthma, or anything stopping you from being the healthiest you. As children of Abba, we can ask for healing and believe we will be healed. Abba sent His Son, Jesus, to die on the cross for us so that we can be healed of our sicknesses.

Isaiah 53:4-5, The Amplified Bible, says,

"He, [Jesus] has carried our sorrows and pains…And by His [Jesus's] stripes (wounds), we are healed."

We are not alone in our sickness and pain because Jesus experienced our pain. More importantly, we have victory over sickness and pain by simply saying, "I am healed in the name of Jesus." When we plead or call the name of Jesus, it reminds Abba; He gave us the name of Jesus to use for our victory. Write down areas where you may feel sick or in pain. Then ask Abba to heal you in the name of Jesus. For example, "Abba, I feel sick with _____. I feel pain with ____ Abba. In the name of Jesus, I receive my healing. By Jesus' stripes, I am healed."

Focus Scripture: Isaiah 53:4-5, The Amplified Bible
"He, [Jesus] has carried our sorrows and pains…And by His [Jesus's] stripes (wounds), we are healed."

Make it personal and say to yourself: I am healed in the name of Jesus! Thank you, Abba, for sending Jesus on the cross for my healing. By Jesus's stripes, I am healed. I believe you have healed me of (say what you need to be healed of) now. I have victory over pain and sickness because you promised to heal me. I claim your healing over my mind, body, spirit, and emotions. I am picturing myself doing what I was not able to do. I see myself being completely healed. Thank you, Abba, for the victory.

Fill in the Scripture:

Isaiah 53:4-5, The Amplified Bible

DAY SEVEN:
I AM!

Who are you? Are you a daughter? A son? A friend? Take a moment to think about who you are. How would you describe yourself? Write it down. We must find our identity or understand who we are through the eyes of Abba. People, places, and things can change, but Abba's love for us will remain the same. Abba says, in Malachi 3:6 New Living Translation, *"I am the Lord; I do not change."*

We must remind ourselves daily who Abba says we are because people can try to convince us we are not who Abba calls us to be. Sometimes, we may even convince ourselves we are not good enough or that we cannot do something. Who we are is not based on what we can do or based on who others say we are. Who we are is who Abba says who we are to Him. This means if we fail today, we are still unique to Him. If we are experiencing hard times, Abba still loves us and has a plan for us.

Focus Scriptures: Jeremiah 29: 11-12, The Amplified Bible
"For I know the plans and thoughts that I have for you,' says the LORD, 'plans for peace and well-being and not for disaster, to give you a future and a hope. Then you will call on Me, and you will come and pray to Me, and I will hear [your voice], and I will listen to you."

Make it personal and say to yourself: I am a child of Abba, God! I am courageous. I am victorious. I embrace who I am with confidence. I am bold; nothing can stand in my way. I am full of faith (belief in Abba and His words). I tell doubt to go away. I am more than a conqueror. I am strong. I am healed. I am loved. I am loving. I am creative. I am smart. I am a genius. I am a good friend. I am Abba's friend. I am at peace. I am forgiven, and I am forgiving. I am accepted. I am unique; Abba sings over me. I am protected; Abba guards me. I am hopeful; Abba has big plans for me! I am powerful; Abba has given me extraordinary power. I am wise; I make good decisions. I am prophetic; Abba shares His secrets with me. I am anointed; Abba has given me special gifting and abilities. I am whom Abba says I am.

Fill in the Scriptures:

Jeremiah 29: 11-12, The Amplified Bible

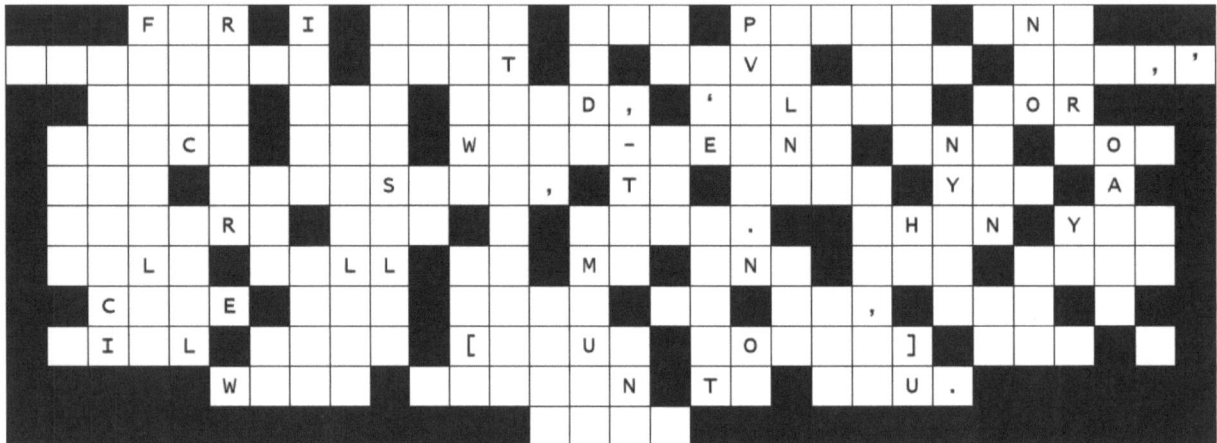

THE END

Congratulations! Yay! You made it to the end! I am so proud of you; you should also be proud of yourself! Continue to seek and speak Abba's words (the Bible) over yourself. As you seek Abba and read the Bible, you will get closer to Abba and learn more about yourself. Abba will show you who you are to Him and all the great gifts He put inside you.

Close your eyes; picture Abba holding you in His arms and carrying you with a smile.

He loves to hear you call Him Abba.